ARCTIC LIGHTS

DEBBIE S. MILLER   ILLUSTRATIONS BY JON VAN ZYLE

ARCTIC NIGHTS

BLOOMSBURY
NEW YORK   LONDON   OXFORD   NEW DELHI   SYDNEY

For my father.
Thanks for all your support over the years.
May you always remember the Land of the Midnight Sun. —Debbie S. Miller

Dedicated to the bright young students whose questions and observations further inspire my art.
—Jon Van Zyle

ACKNOWLEDGMENTS

A special thanks goes to my editor, Emily Easton, for encouraging me to write a book about Alaska's changing light.
I'm also grateful to Judy Triplehorn, an invaluable resource at the University of Alaska's Geophysical Institute; Dr. Neil Davis, who helped me better understand the dynamics of our northern light; and the National Weather Service staff in Fairbanks, who provided light and temperature information. Last, many thanks to all of my writing colleagues with the Fairbanks Society of Children's Book Writers and Illustrators.

First published in the United States of America in 2003 by Walker Books for Young Readers,
an imprint of Bloomsbury Publishing, Inc.
Paperback edition published in 2007
www.bloomsbury.com

Bloomsbury is a registered trademark of Bloomsbury Publishing Plc

For information about permission to reproduce selections from this book, write to Permissions,
Bloomsbury Children's Books, 1385 Broadway,
New York, New York 10018

Bloomsbury books may be purchased for business or promotional use. For information on bulk purchases please contact Macmillan Corporate and Premium Sales Department at specialmarkets@macmillan.com

The artist used acrylic on Masonite panels to create the illustrations for this book.

Book design by Maura Fadden Rosenthal/Mspace

The Library of Congress has cataloged the hardcover edition as follows:
Miller, Debbie S.
Arctic lights, arctic nights / Debbie S. Miller ; illustrations by Jon Van Zyle.
p. cm.
Summary: Describes the unique light phenomena of the Alaskan Arctic and the way animals adapt to the temperature and daylight changes each month of the year.
ISBN-10: 0-8027-8856-4 • ISBN-13: 978-0-8027-8856-6 (hardcover)
ISBN-10: 0-8027-8857-2 • ISBN-13: 978-0-8027-8857-3 (reinforced)
1. Zoology—Arctic regions—Juvenile literature. 2. Arctic regions—Climate—Juvenile literature.
[1. Zoology—Arctic regions. 2. Arctic regions.] I. Van Zyle, Jon. II. Title.
QL104.M45 2003   591.4'0911'3—dc21   2002191047

ISBN-10: 0-8027-9636-2 • ISBN-13: 978-0-8027-9636-3 (paperback)

Printed in China by C&C Offset Printing Co., Ltd., Shenzhen, Guangdong
20 19 18 17 16 15 14

All papers used by Bloomsbury Publishing, Inc., are natural, recyclable products made from wood grown in well-managed forests. The manufacturing processes conform to the environmental regulations of the country of origin.

INTRODUCTION

During my travels to schools across America, many children have asked me questions about the dynamics of light in Alaska and the Arctic. Is it dark in Alaska all the time? What are the northern lights, and who turns them on? How do you sleep in the summer if it's always light? These questions inspired me to write a book about light in Alaska and how it changes from month to month.

Alaska is a vast state. The amount of light and snowfall and the range in temperatures have extreme variations, depending on where you stand. If you live in Barrow, Alaska's northernmost Inupiat community, you experience eighty-four days of continuous light during summer, but in winter there is no direct sunshine for sixty-seven days. If you live in a more southerly location, such as Juneau or Ketchikan, you do not experience twenty-four-hour daylight or the complete loss of sun. The amount of light above the Arctic Circle, the latitude where one first begins to see a never-setting sun, is very different than the amount of light farther south.

Our family lives in Fairbanks, Alaska's second largest city. Fairbanks lies in the heart of our state, about 115 miles south of the Arctic Circle. This seasonal description of Alaska is based on the light and average temperatures of Fairbanks. Although the sun sets here for a few hours during the summer, we still experience constant light as the sun falls only a few degrees below the horizon. During winter, we lose direct sunshine for much of the day, but we have long periods of twilight, when you can see outside. It is never completely dark all day long. Even places such as Barrow experience several hours of twilight during their sunless days.

The light of Alaska and the Arctic is dynamic and beautiful, from its midnight sun colors and dancing northern lights to its lingering twilight and pink alpenglow. This book is a team effort to describe the beauty, drama, and unusual features of our changing light of the Far North.

Splash . . . drip. A cow moose dunks her head and clips off some lily pads. Her calf splashes through the water behind her. Across the lake a pair of trumpeter swans dabble for food. In the evening, mosquitoes softly whine, and the songs of thrushes drift through the cooling air.

On summer solstice, the top of the world tilts toward the sun. Light and new life flood the land. During this longest day of the year, the sun shines brightly for all but a few hours. The midnight sun briefly hides behind the tallest mountains, but there is no darkness.

July 21   19 hours and 24 minutes of daylight

Hop . . . hop . . . pause. A snowshoe hare scampers across a meadow near the edge of the forest. She wears a summer coat that blends with the color of the earth. Her month-old hare nibbles on a blade of grass and is ready to live on its own.

The days grow shorter, but there is still no darkness. The sun just hides a little longer below the northern horizon. Sunset colors linger until the sun rises again and follows a circular path around the top of the spinning world.

Sik-sik-sik-sik-sik!! A ground squirrel warns other squirrels that grizzlies are near. Like the mother bear and her cubs, the squirrels are busy feeding on plants to get fat so they can survive the long winter.

The sun drops lower on the horizon. Darkness has returned, and nights bring the first frost. About seven minutes of daylight slip away each day. With shorter days and temperatures falling, many birds feel the urge to migrate south.

September 21 Fall equinox 12 hours and 22 minutes of daylight

Garrr . . . TROOa. The last of the sandhill cranes gather together. They grow restless on this blustery day. With long-legged steps, they pump their huge wings toward the setting sun. Their trumpeting calls rattle through the cold sky.

The fall equinox marks the end of summer and the time when there is an equal amount of lightness and darkness. Within a few days, the nights will grow longer than the days, and temperatures will seldom rise above freezing.

October 21 9 hours and 2 minutes of daylight

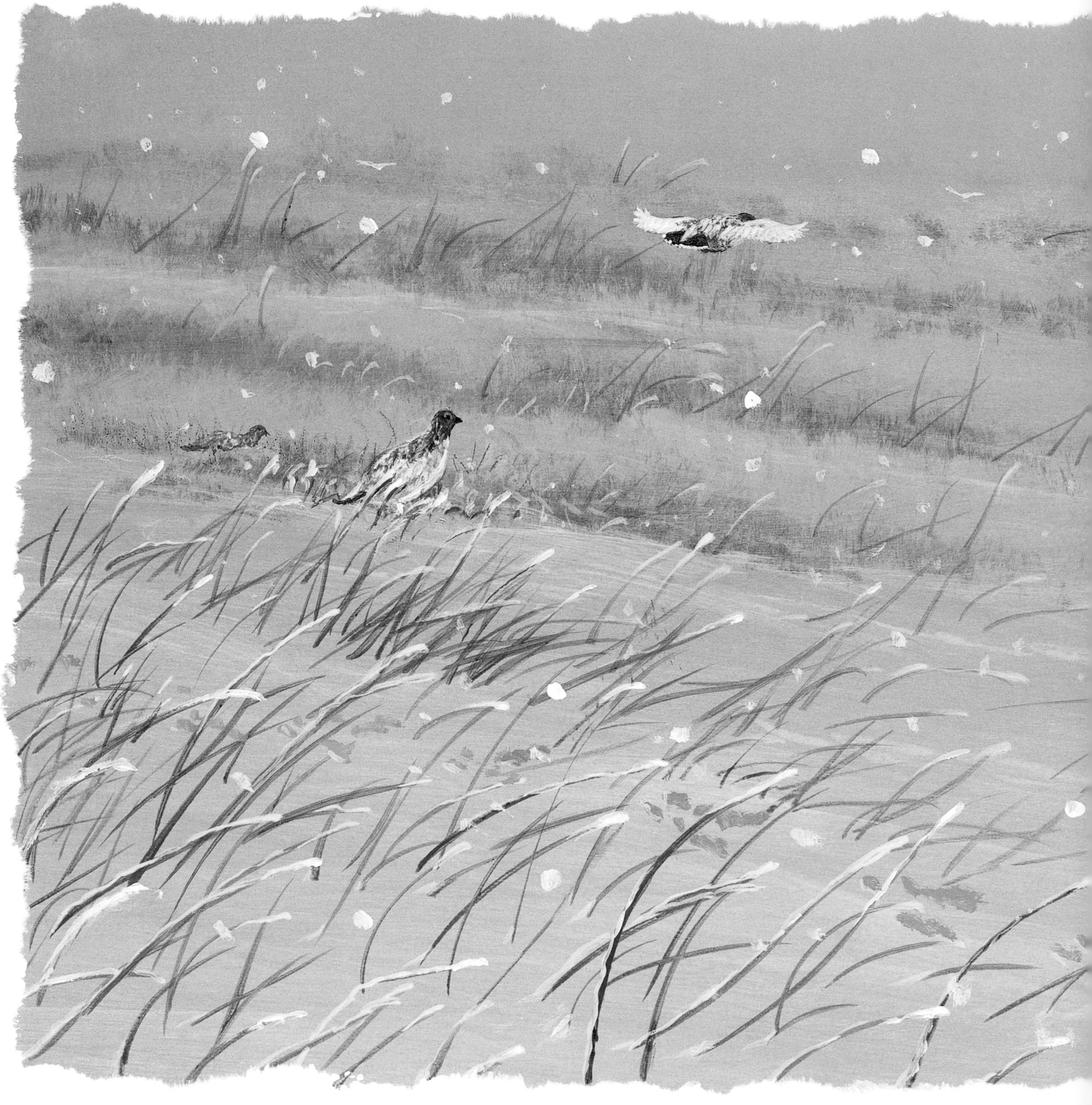

Clack . . . clatter. Bull caribou fight for their mates. Head to head, they lock antlers through a veil of snow. Tracks appear again, showing the daily journeys of snowshoe hare and ptarmigan. They wear new white coats to match their snowy world.

The sun's arc drops lower as the top of the world angles away from its source of heat. White sky and earth create flat light, and it is difficult to see where land ends and sky begins.

Ah-rooooooo. A lone wolf howls to its mate on a ridge above the valley. His warm breath frosts his whiskers and eyelashes. As the temperature falls below zero, the lake ice cracks and moans.

A full moon rises, and the snow glitters. Although the nights are much longer, the moonlight reflects off the snow, making the forest appear lighter than in September, when there was no snow.

Hush . . . silence. Temperatures may fall to 40 degrees below zero. In the twilight, the moose nibble on twigs and bark to survive the winter. As the Alaska-blue sky grows dark, they bed down in the powdery snow.

On winter solstice, the top of the world tilts away from the sun. The nights are long, and the cold runs deep. During this shortest day of the year, a family bundles up and watches nature's holiday celebration. The magical northern lights dance and swirl across the clear, icy sky.

Hop . . . hop. A snowshoe hare scampers softly along her trail on quiet furry feet.
Only her dark eyes reveal a white-camouflaged body.

The sun climbs thumb-high above the southern horizon, casting long, dark shadows across the snow. Days grow a little longer, but there is still no warmth. As the sun rolls beneath the horizon, the soft pink alpenglow bathes the snowy mountains.

Toss . . . turn. Bears and ground squirrel are hibernating in their cozy dens.
The ground squirrel shifts his position to control body temperature. Mother bear and
her cubs nestle together for several months beneath the snow.

   Nights grow shorter. Each day brings seven to eight minutes more light, and the
sun begins to feel warm. In the low-angle sunshine, snow crystals become tiny
prisms, scattering the light. Bright sparkles show the colors of the rainbow. As the
sun climbs higher, the snow is sprinkled with glints, colorless crystals that reflect the
sun's rays like miniature mirrors.

Crawk . . .Crawk. A pair of ravens tumble and roll in the sky. Their black wings glisten in the bright light. Spring is in the air, yet night and morning temperatures are still below freezing. Diamond dust magically forms above the valley as moist air turns into ice crystals.

There is another natural phenomenon. Two bright "sun dogs"
appear in the cirrus clouds on either side of the sun. As light passes
through the ice-laced clouds, two small "suns" form with colorful halos around
them. This day marks the beginning of spring, the vernal equinox. There is an equal
amount of light and darkness, but soon the days will grow longer than the nights.

Drip . . . trickle. The snow and ice are melting, and each day brings more light and warmer temperatures. Cumulus clouds billow above the land. The underside of a cloud reflects a changing world. These reflections, or blinks, show the darkness of open water and forests or the lightness of snow and ice.

Longer days signal animals to begin their migrations. Caribou herds move toward their calving grounds. The trumpeter swans come back to their old nests.

Sunrise: 3:07 A.M.   Sunset: 10:31 P.M.   Average high: 59°F   Average low: 39°F

Tseet-tseet. The music of songbirds has returned. Nights and snow in the lowlands have vanished! Rivers flow once again. The world is green. Dappled light dances on the sticky new leaves of the birch and aspen trees.

Near the entrance to their den, wolf pups tussle together while their mother basks in the sunshine. The father wolf catches the scent of caribou and trots up the river to find his prey.

June 21 Summer solstice

Once again the endless June days have returned, and light drenches the great wilderness. In the Land of the Midnight Sun, the magical light and explosion of life go hand in hand.

GLOSSARY

Spring

Alpenglow: A reddish or pinkish glow seen on snow-covered mountains near the time of sunrise or sunset. Alpenglow colors vary from red and pink to lilac and purple. In polar regions, alpenglow can extend for prolonged periods when the sun lingers just below the horizon.

Blinks: The underside of a cloud often absorbs the reflection of sunlight from the Earth's surface. The cloud base appears dark when it shows the reflections of land, forest, and water. Cloud bases appear light when they show reflections of snow and ice. When the clouds reveal the presence of unseen water, this condition is termed *water sky*.

Diamond dust: When moist air enters a clear, cold air mass, tiny ice crystals form. These crystals, known as diamond dust, glitter as they fall through the sky. Diamond dust appears magical, as though the snowy world is shrouded in fairy dust.

Summer

Fall equinox: This day marks the end of summer and the beginning of autumn. The word *equinox* comes from the French words *equi* (equal) and *nox* (night). On the fall equinox, the days and nights are of equal length. The fall equinox usually occurs around the twenty-first day of September, the time when the sun's position crosses the equator as the Earth follows its circular path around the sun. The nights soon grow longer than the days.

Flat light: Flat light conditions occur when the land and sky are largely white due to snow conditions, fog, or clouds. Sky and earth merge together, and it is difficult to see any relief or depth of your surroundings. The world appears to be one continuous white surface.

Glints: Glints are colorless points of light that reflect off the faces of ice crystals. Glints occur at any angle relative to the sun, so they are more commonly seen than the colorful sparkles. Flashes of sunlight that reflect off water are also known as glints.

Midnight sun: Above the Arctic Circle (latitudes higher than 66.5 degrees), the sun can be seen at midnight during the summer. The midnight sun rolls along the northern horizon, casting beautiful sunrise and sunset colors. The Land of the Midnight Sun magically glows from the low-angle light and never-setting sun.

Winter

Northern lights: The aurora (also known as the aurora borealis in the Northern Hemisphere and the aurora australis in the Southern Hemisphere) are multicolored lights that glow at night, primarily at high latitudes. The aurora can vary in color from greenish yellow to violet and red. These magical lights form curtains, bands, waves, and long, straight rays as they swirl through the sky. The lights occur when fast-moving charged particles from the sun mix with other gases in the upper atmosphere above the Earth's magnetic field.

Sparkles: Sparkles are colorful sprinkles of light that appear in the snow. Sparkles are most frequently seen in freshly fallen snow or in frost when the crystals are about 22 degrees from the sun. The ice crystals act as tiny prisms, breaking the light into the colors of the rainbow. This broken light is also known as refracted light.

Summer solstice: The word *solstice* comes from the French words *sol* (sun), and *status,* (to come to a stop). Summer solstice traditionally marks the end of spring and the beginning of summer. In the Northern Hemisphere, summer solstice falls around the twenty-first day of June, the longest day

Fall

of the year. On this day, the top of the world tilts toward the sun to its maximum extent. In Alaska and the Arctic, this means there are twenty-four hours of light, and no darkness. This continual light lasts for two or more months.

Sun dogs: Sun dogs, or parhelia, often form in pairs on either side of the sun. These bright, colorful spots of light are usually reddish on the side facing the sun. Bluish white streams of light often extend away from the spots. Sun dogs often form in cirrus clouds where ice crystals are present. As light bends through a patch of ice crystals, sun dogs appear. This refracted light is sometimes associated with bright halos that encircle the sun.

Twilight: This is the period of time when the sun is below the horizon but still illuminates the sky so that one can see outside. Dusk refers to the twilight time after sunset, and dawn refers to the twilight period before sunrise. Polar regions have long periods of twilight because of the Earth's tilt and curvature. In December, places like Alaska receive the most twilight, with three or more hours of indirect light each day. The sky gradually turns to a deep midnight blue, the color of the Alaska flag.

Vernal equinox: The word *vernal* means spring. On the vernal equinox, the days and nights are once again of equal length. The vernal equinox usually occurs around the twenty-first day of March, marking the end of winter and the beginning of spring. The days soon grow longer than the nights.

Winter solstice: In the Northern Hemisphere, winter solstice traditionally falls around the twenty-first day of December, the shortest day of the year. On this day, the top of the world tilts away from the sun to its maximum extent. In the northernmost parts of Alaska, above the Arctic Circle, the winter sun does not rise above the horizon for more than two months. While there is no direct sunshine in these locations, there are several hours of twilight each day as the sun is just below the horizon.